THE AMAZING BOOK OF MAZES

WILD GUESS

www.wildguess.co

ISBN-13: 978-1950601066
ISBN-10: 1950601064

INTRODUCTION

Mazes require focus, especially these ones.

Look carefully – some have multiple entrances, some have multiple exits, and some have both.

It's more common to enter from the bottom and exit out the top, but each maze is designed to flow well from either direction. While I recommend using highlighters to solve the mazes, be careful about any bleeding ink.

Thanks for checking these mazes out, I hope you enjoy them!

Apologies in advance if you have bad eyesight.

a little tight

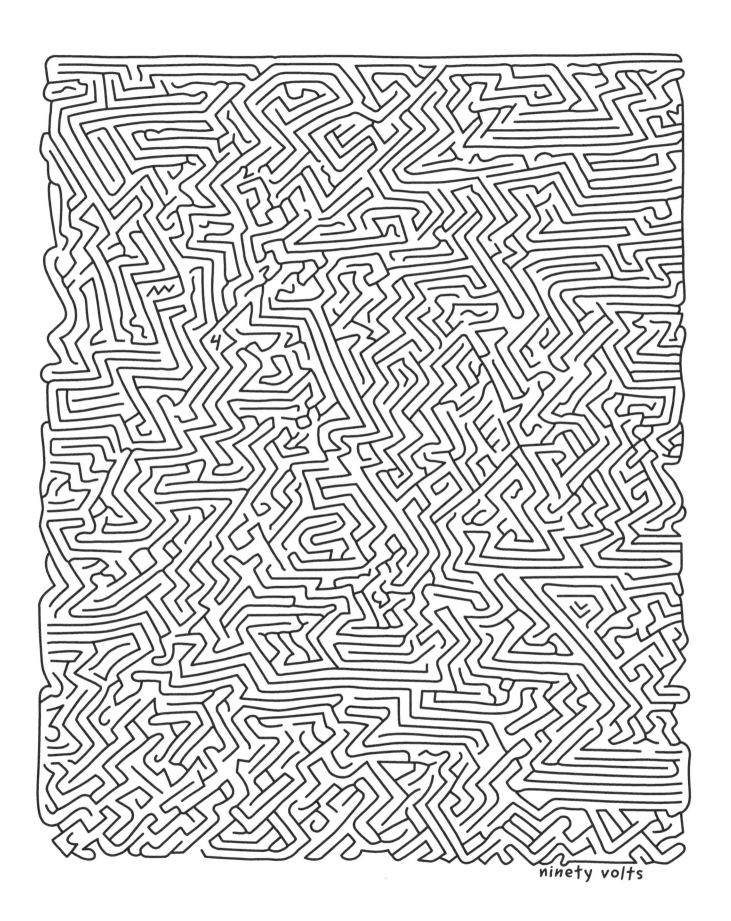

ninety volts

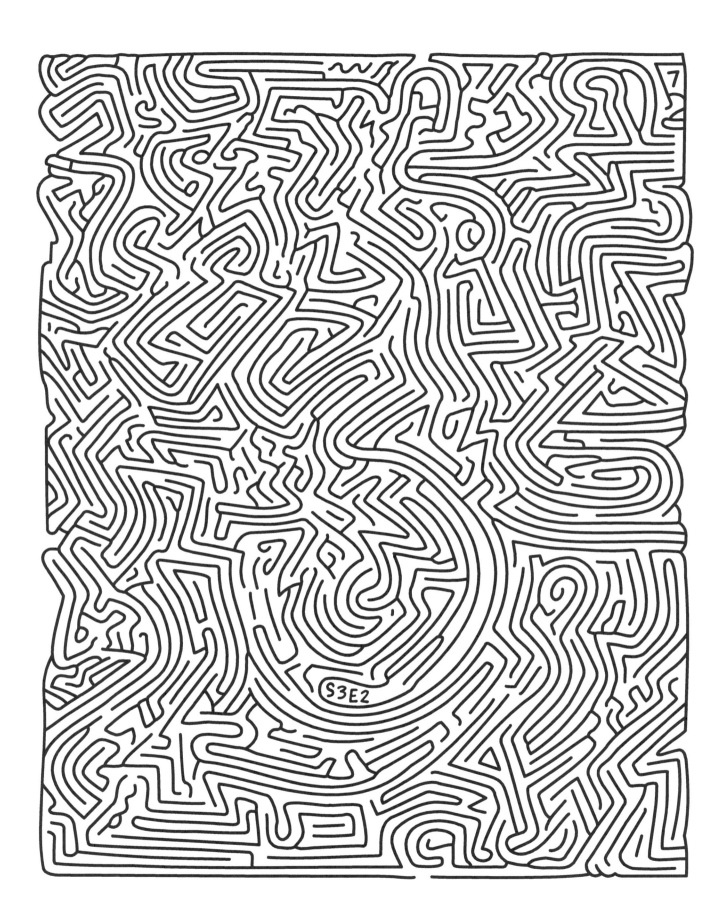

Forden

BONUS

CAN YOU FIND THE FOLLOWING PIECES IN THE MAZE ABOVE?

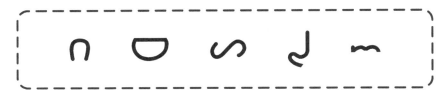

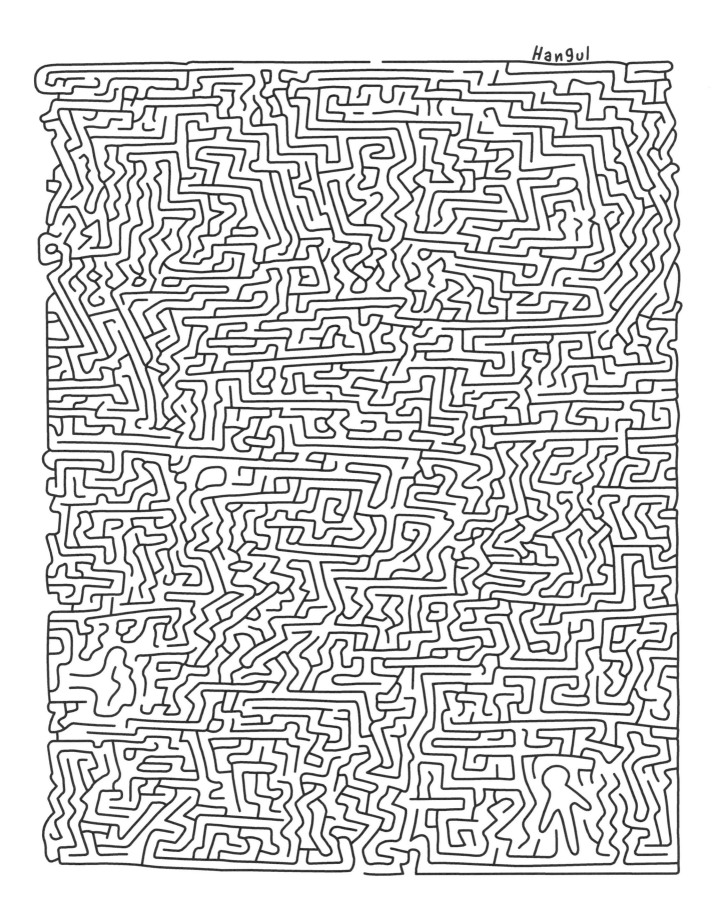
Hangul

the bends

catagories

piled limes

fortitude

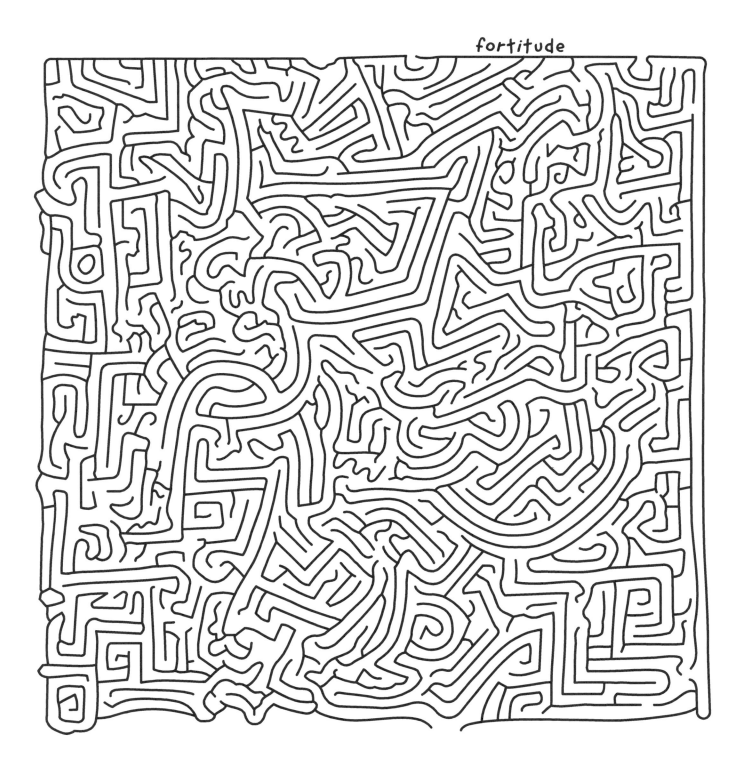

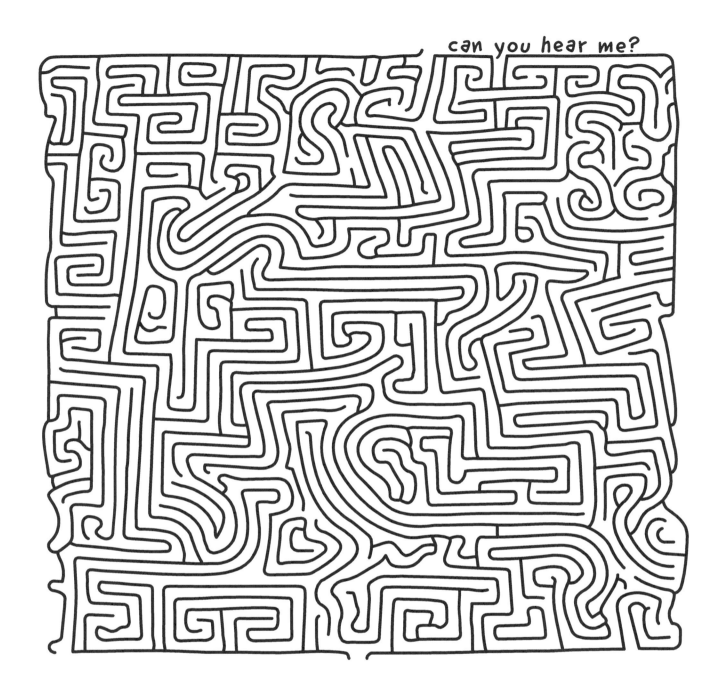

can you hear me?

BONUS

CAN YOU FIND THE FOLLOWING PIECES IN THE MAZE ABOVE?

BONUS

(HOW MANY TOTAL PIECES IN THE MAZE ABOVE?)

BONUS

CAN YOU FIND THE FOLLOWING PIECES IN THE MAZE ABOVE?

operation

frame data

cheese for a mall rat

street Performer

tofu scramble

candelabra

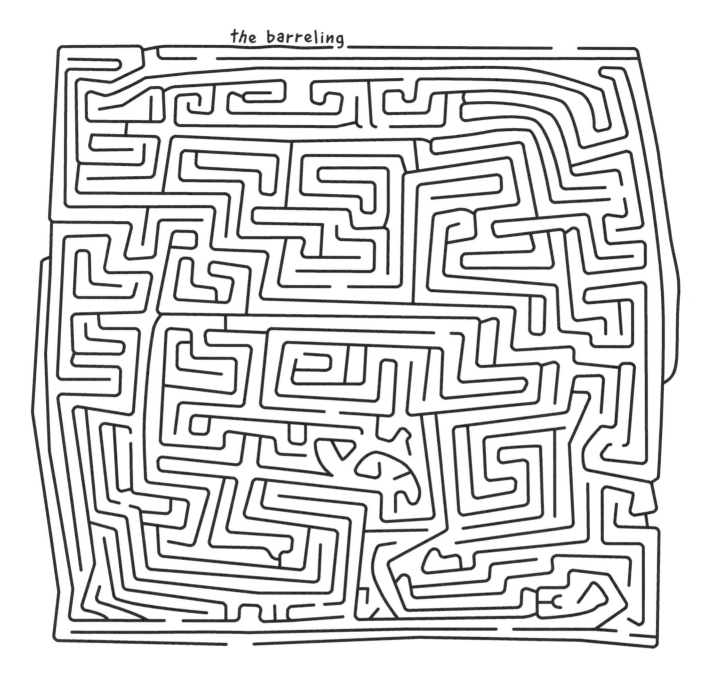

the barreling _____

BONUS

CAN YOU FIND THE FOLLOWING PIECES IN THE MAZE ABOVE?

the boring one

BONUS

CAN YOU FIND THE FOLLOWING PIECES IN THE MAZE ABOVE?

chicken little

paper tiger

shēng

BONUS

CAN YOU FIND THE FOLLOWING PIECES IN THE MAZE ABOVE?

mists and meridians

caped crusaders

Quarries

BONUS

CAN YOU FIND THE FOLLOWING PIECES IN THE MAZE ABOVE?

on the take

double dash

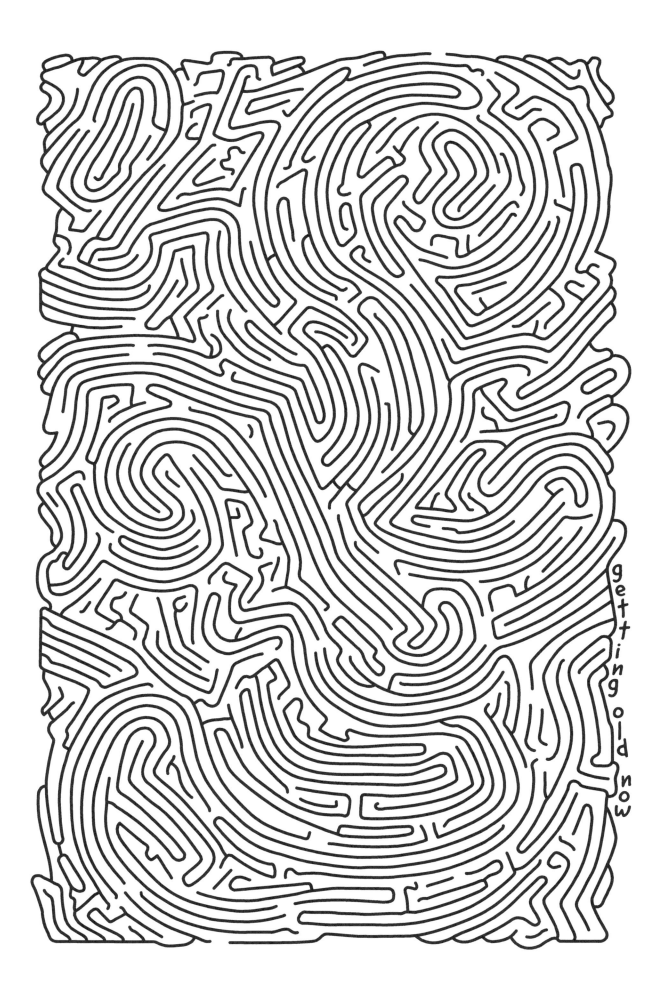

the dance

Human

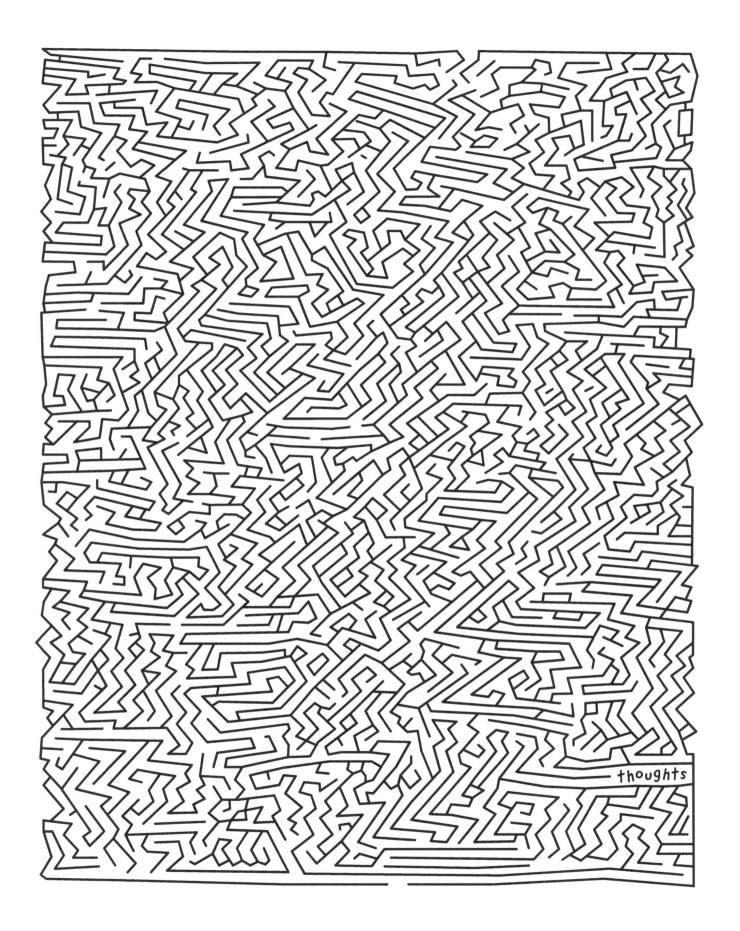

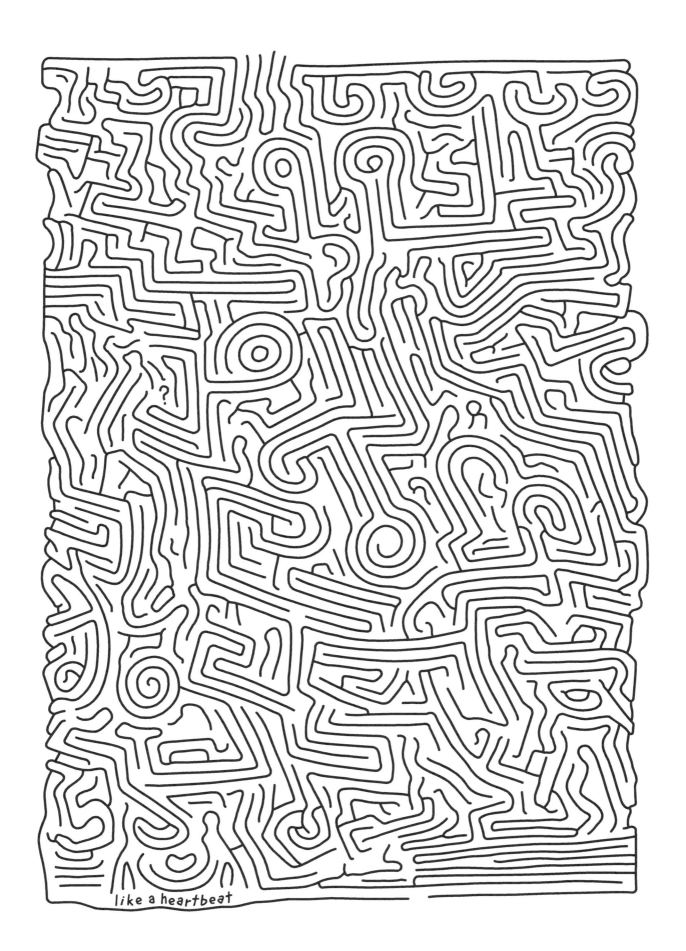

like a heartbeat

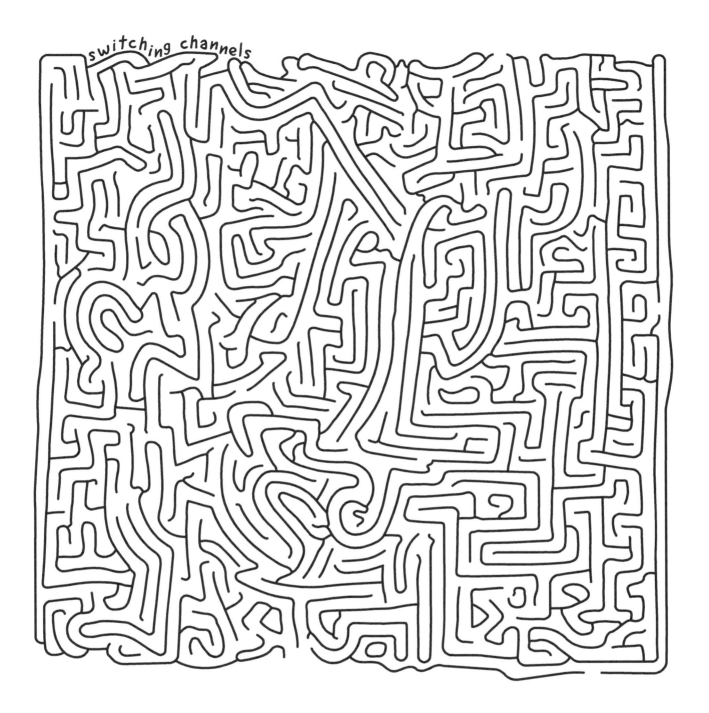

switching channels

BONUS

CAN YOU FIND THE FOLLOWING PIECES IN THE MAZE ABOVE?

Chip's Challenge

it's all an illusion

a houseboat on the Grijalva

live on Twitch

conniption

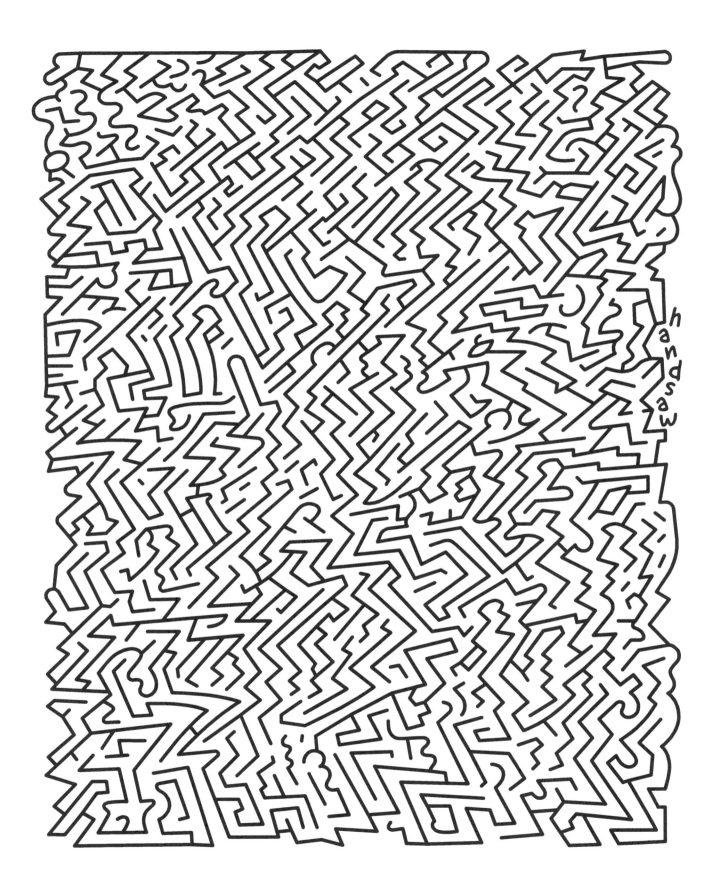

ringing in the new year

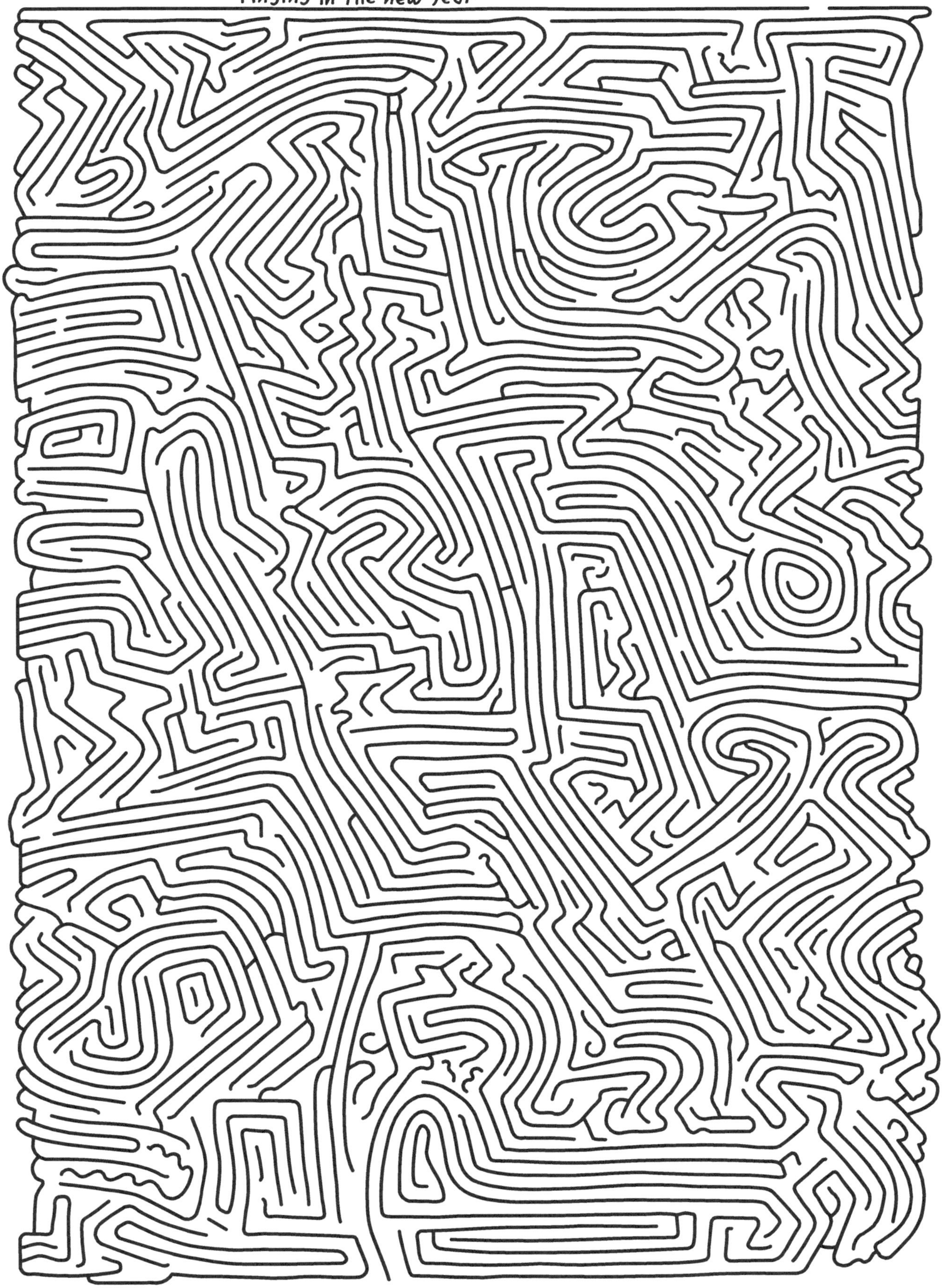

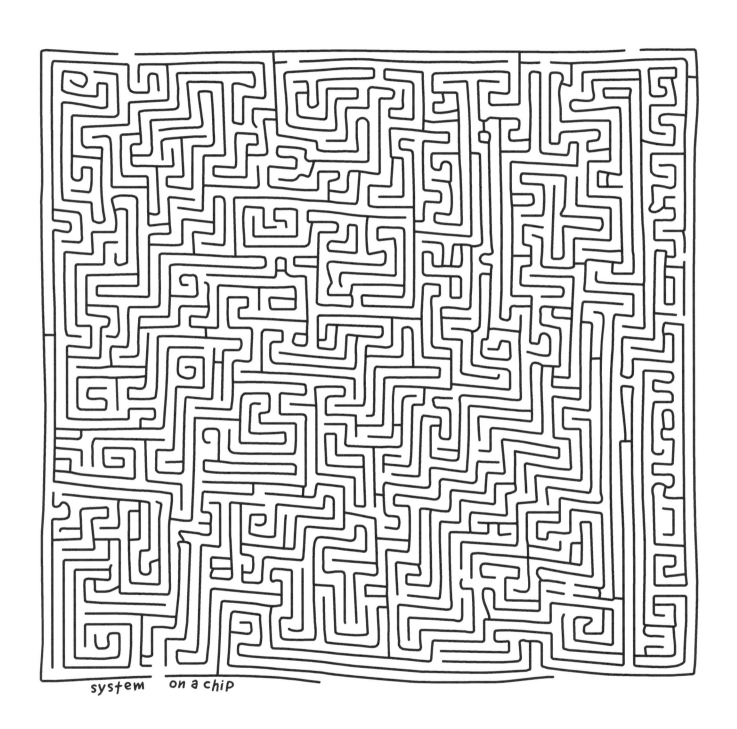

system on a chip

a bank creed

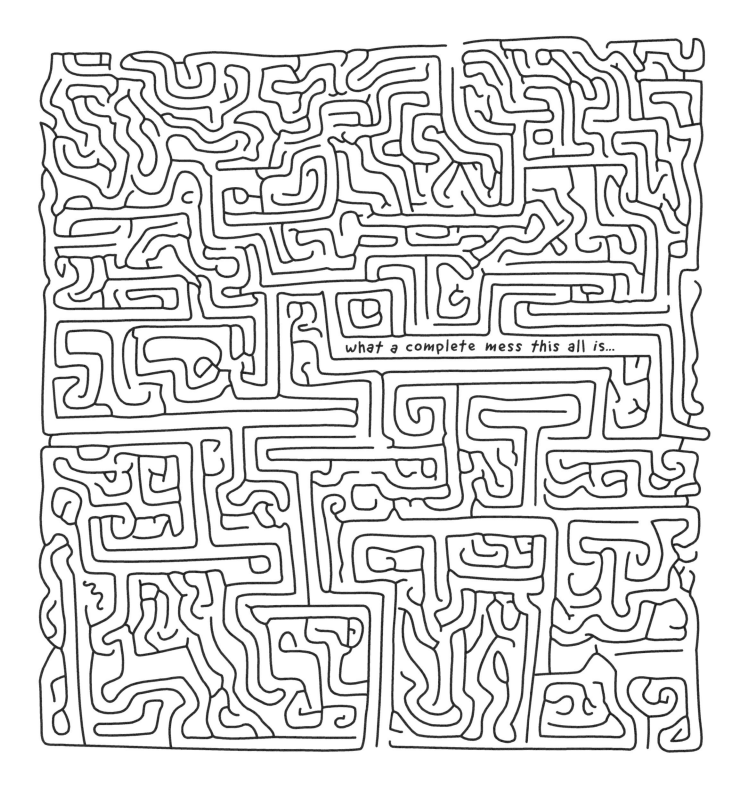

ski season

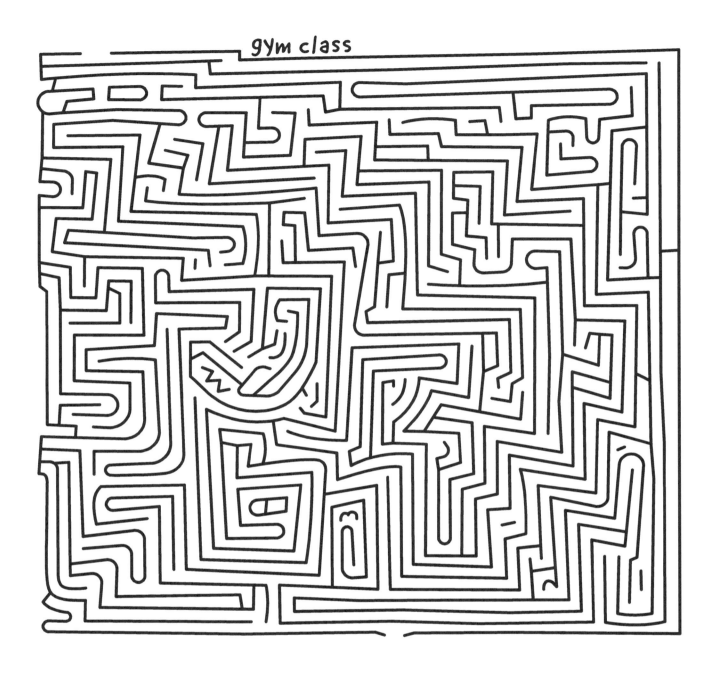

gym class

BONUS

CAN YOU FIND THE FOLLOWING PIECES IN THE MAZE ABOVE?

for Celeste

BONUS

CAN YOU FIND THE FOLLOWING PIECES IN THE MAZE ABOVE?

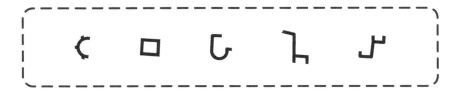

the ascent

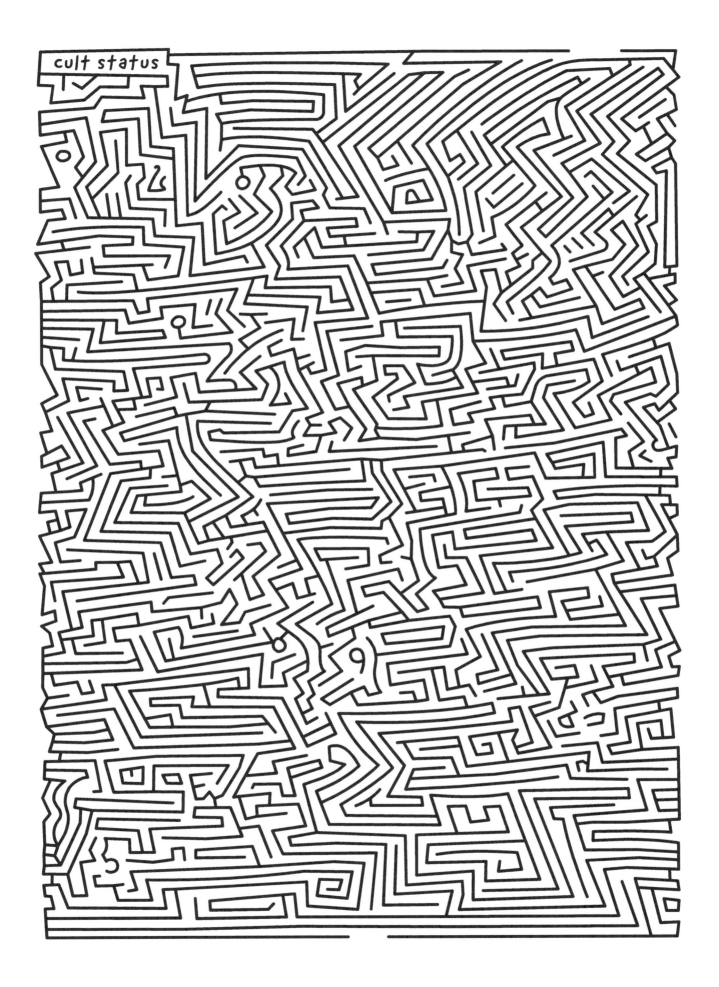

ONE FINAL BONUS

THE TWENTY OBJECTS BELOW ARE ALL PIECES FROM THE MAZES
INSIDE THIS BOOK. CAN YOU GO BACK AND FIND THEM ALL?

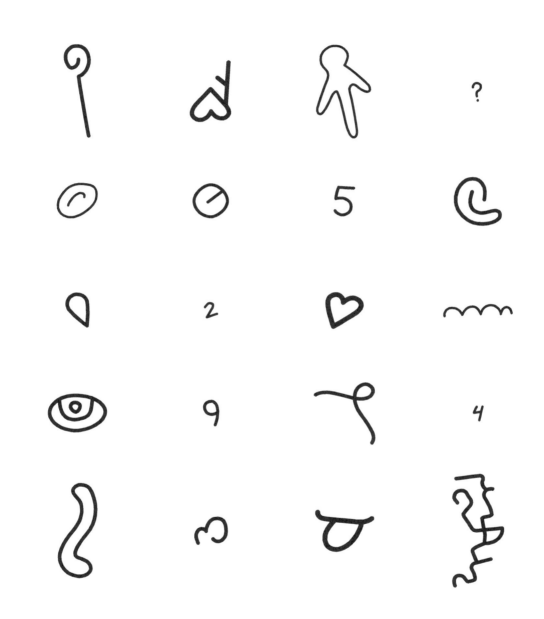

(NONE OF THE PIECES HAVE BEEN ROTATED OR SCALED, SO THEY SHOULD
APPEAR ROUGHLY IDENTICAL ON THIS PAGE AS THEY DO IN THE MAZES)

THANK YOU!

If you've made it this far, thanks.

And if you enjoyed the book, please scan the QR code below and leave me a review!

Made in United States
Troutdale, OR
06/27/2025